Turning Points
of the
American Revolution

By John Hamilton

VISIT US AT
WWW.ABDOPUBLISHING.COM

Printed in the United States of America, North Mankato, Minnesota.
122012
012013

 PRINTED ON RECYCLED PAPER

Editor: Sue Hamilton
Graphic Design: Sue Hamilton
Cover Design: Neil Klinepier
Cover: Painting by Don Troiani, www.historicalartprints.com
Interior Photos and Illustrations: AP-pgs 14-15; Brown University Library-pg 12; Corbis-pgs
16 & 21; Getty Images-pgs 18 & 25; Granger Collection-pgs 1, 19, 26 & 27; John Hamilton-pgs
10, 13, 17, 20, 22 & 24; Military and Historical Image Bank-pgs 3, 8-9, 11 & 28; Metropolitan
Museum of Art (Emanuel Leutze artist)-pgs 4-5; Museum of the American Revolution-pg 6;
National Park Service-Base Maps on pgs 22 & 24; U.S. Army Center of Military History-pgs 7,
23 & 29.

ABDO Booklinks
To learn more about the American Revolution, visit ABDO Publishing Company online. Web
sites about the American Revolution are featured on our Book Links pages. These links are
routinely monitored and updated to provide the most current information available.
Web site: www.abdopublishing.com

Library of Congress Control Number: 2012945984

Cataloging-in-Publication Data

Hamilton, John.
 Turning points of the American Revolution / John Hamilton.
  p. cm. -- (American Revolution)
Includes index.
ISBN 978-1-61783-682-4
1. United States--History--Revolution, 1775-1783--Campaigns--Juvenile literature.
I. Title.
973.3--dc22
                                                              2012945984

CONTENTS

Troops from the Hesse-Cassel Jaeger Corps. Commonly called "Hessians," these German soldiers were paid mercenaries who fought for the British during the American Revolution.

THE BATTLE OF TRENTON

George Washington takes his army across the Delaware River.

As 1776 drew to a close, the American Continental Army, commanded by General George Washington, found itself on the brink of total defeat. In August, Washington had organized a brilliant and surprising retreat from the disastrous Battle of Long Island, which kept his army intact. But ever since, he had fought one losing battle after another. New York City was now in the hands of the British Army, commanded by General William Howe.

Washington's army was exhausted, poorly equipped, and slipping into despair. Soldiers deserted in droves. The Patriot dream of a free and independent United States was slipping away.

After occupying New York City, General Howe ordered his best field commander, General Charles Cornwallis, to hunt down and destroy what was left of Washington's army. After a long cat-and-mouse chase across New Jersey, Cornwallis finally caught up to the Americans on December 8, but it was too late. The entire Continental Army had crossed the Delaware River into Pennsylvania.

General Cornwallis's prey was maddeningly close. The British searched for a way to cross the river, but Washington had ordered all boats destroyed for miles along the shore. Cornwallis was stuck, and freezing weather was setting in.

In those days, it was very hard to fight during the winter months. Weapons malfunctioned, frostbite injured the troops, and food was always scarce. Most armies went into "winter quarters" and waited until spring to resume fighting.

General Cornwallis decided to station his troops at several forts and towns along the New Jersey side of the Delaware River. One of those British outposts was the village of Trenton, New Jersey. It was commanded by Colonel Johann Rall, who led about 1,500 Hessian troops. The Hessians were paid soldiers (mercenaries) from today's Germany. They were battle-hardened veterans. Even though Cornwallis warned them to stay on guard, the Hessian troops felt they had little to fear from the inexperienced Patriot army. Colonel Rall called them "country clowns."

On the Pennsylvania side of the Delaware River, the demoralized Patriot troops badly needed a victory. George Washington made a bold decision. He would use the element of surprise to cross the river at night and attack the British when they least expected it.

After sunset on Christmas Day, December 25, 1776, George Washington gathered his army. The weather was terrible. A cold wind blew through the poorly equipped soldiers's thin uniforms. Some wore rags on their feet. Despite the hardships, few complained.

General Cornwallis

Under cover of darkness, the army began crossing the river. Large Durham boats carried 18 heavy cannons. A blinding snowstorm and ice-choked water made the voyage hazardous. Only a portion of the Patriot army made it safely across. They gathered themselves, and by 4:00 a.m. on December 26, about 2,400 American troops, led by George Washington himself, began trudging several miles south toward Trenton.

At 8:00 a.m., as the faint sun rose over the New Jersey countryside, the Patriots reached their goal. Most of the Hessians were asleep in their barracks, having celebrated Christmas the day before. Suddenly, shots rang out.

At first, the Hessian troops were surprised and disorganized. They quickly put up a fierce defense, but it was too late. George Washington led his troops bravely into battle, calling out, "March on, my brave fellows, after me!"

George Washington's troops enter Trenton, New Jersey, on December 26, 1776.

Hessian troops occupying Trenton, New Jersey, did not expect a battle with George Washington's Continental Army on December 26, 1776. The surprise attack resulted in a much-needed Patriot victory.

In less than an hour, Hessian Colonel Rall lay mortally wounded in the snow, and his troops were forced to surrender.

At the end of the brief battle, the British side suffered 40 killed, 66 wounded, and 918 captured. Just 4 Patriots were killed, and another 8 wounded. The Americans captured many horses, cannons, muskets, and ammunition, which were all badly needed.

Morale among the Patriots soared after the bold attack on Trenton. Fewer soldiers deserted, and enlistments in the Continental Army increased. Perhaps there was some life yet in this Patriot army.

January 3, 1777

THE BATTLE OF PRINCETON

After the lopsided victory at the Battle of Trenton in New Jersey, General George Washington moved his troops across the Delaware River back into Pennsylvania to rest and re-supply. He suspected that British General Charles Cornwallis would soon move to punish the Americans for their sneak attack. In fact, Cornwallis had left his base at Princeton, New Jersey, and was on the road toward Trenton with 6,700 Redcoats, all eager for revenge.

Washington moved his army once more across the river and set up defensive positions south of Trenton.

News of the Patriot victory at Trenton had spread through the countryside, and reinforcements swelled Washington's ranks. The two armies set up positions across from each other, ready for battle. But instead of fighting Cornwallis on his own terms, Washington made another surprising move. On the night of January 2, most of the Patriots slipped away, leaving a small force behind with campfires lit to trick the British into thinking the main army was still in camp.

On January 3, Washington's 4,600-man army attacked Princeton, which was defended by only 1,200 Redcoats left behind by Cornwallis. A fierce battle raged, but the Patriots won the day, losing only 23 men killed and 20 wounded. The British lost 28 killed, 58 wounded, and nearly 200 captured.

Just eight days after the Battle of Trenton, a second Patriot victory came on January 3, 1777, at Princeton, New Jersey.

The Battle of Princeton was a stunning British defeat. When he received the news, General Cornwallis rushed back to the city. To his frustration, the American army had already melted away.

By January 6, Washington and his troops found safe refuge in Morristown, New Jersey, where they set up winter quarters. With the victories in Trenton and Princeton, in less than two weeks's time the Patriots had driven the British from southern New Jersey, in winter, with troops that were ill-equipped and outnumbered. Morale among the Americans soared, and enlistments increased. The British realized to their dismay that the American Revolution was far from over.

September 11, 1777

THE BATTLE OF BRANDYWINE

During the first months of 1777, George Washington and the American Continental Army regrouped and resupplied in Morristown, New Jersey. Morristown was an ideal spot for winter quarters. Its high ground was easily defended, and the Patriots could keep track of enemy movements at the British headquarters in occupied New York City, which was only about 30 miles (48 km) away.

Great Britain, meanwhile, devised a plan to stop the American rebellion once and for all. General John Burgoyne would take a large army from Canada into New England,

splitting the northern colonies. General William Howe, commander in chief of British forces in North America, would attack the rebel capital at Philadelphia, Pennsylvania, home of the Continental Congress.

The British plan was a bold, two-pronged assault, but it depended on Howe eventually moving north to help Burgoyne in New England. Howe, however, was not very concerned with the northern campaign. He badly wanted to crush the Patriots in one fell swoop by capturing Philadelphia. He also wanted to collect the glory that would come from defeating George Washington in open battle.

General William Howe

12

The Patriot army blocked the way between New York and Philadelphia. During the spring and summer months of 1777, General Howe tried to draw Washington out of his New Jersey stronghold, but the Patriot general never took the bait. Instead of committing his entire army in these small skirmishes, Washington was content to keep Howe bottled up in New York.

Finally, on July 8, 1777, General Howe loaded 16,500 Redcoats onto 265 Royal Navy ships and set sail. His plan was to attack the rebel capital from the south. Six weeks later, his massive army arrived in upper Chesapeake Bay, at Head of Elk, Maryland. By September 9, Howe's troops had marched overland well into Pennsylvania.

The British Assault on Philadelphia, 1777

NEW YORK
CT
New York City
NEW JERSEY
PENNSYLVANIA
Battle of Brandywine
Philadelphia
Head of Elk
MARYLAND
WV
DE
VIRGINIA
Chesapeake Bay
Atlantic Ocean
N
American Forces
British Forces

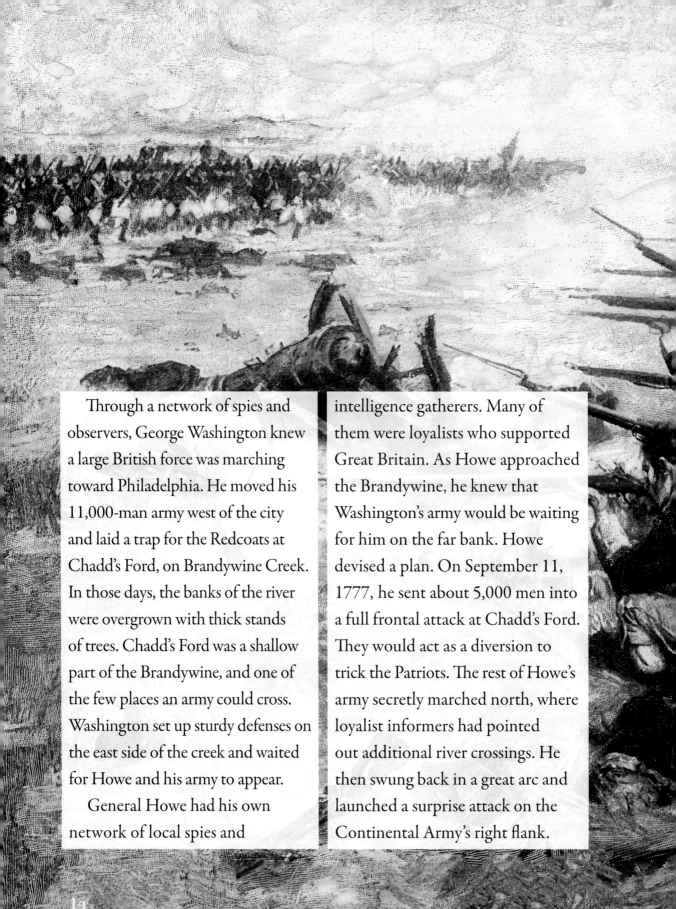

Through a network of spies and observers, George Washington knew a large British force was marching toward Philadelphia. He moved his 11,000-man army west of the city and laid a trap for the Redcoats at Chadd's Ford, on Brandywine Creek. In those days, the banks of the river were overgrown with thick stands of trees. Chadd's Ford was a shallow part of the Brandywine, and one of the few places an army could cross. Washington set up sturdy defenses on the east side of the creek and waited for Howe and his army to appear.

General Howe had his own network of local spies and intelligence gatherers. Many of them were loyalists who supported Great Britain. As Howe approached the Brandywine, he knew that Washington's army would be waiting for him on the far bank. Howe devised a plan. On September 11, 1777, he sent about 5,000 men into a full frontal attack at Chadd's Ford. They would act as a diversion to trick the Patriots. The rest of Howe's army secretly marched north, where loyalist informers had pointed out additional river crossings. He then swung back in a great arc and launched a surprise attack on the Continental Army's right flank.

Americans held their ground early in the Battle of the Brandywine, on September 11, 1777. They were later outmaneuvered and outgunned, but remained determined to defeat the British Army.

F. C. YOHN

Redcoats fire at Patriot troops during a reenactment of the Battle of Brandywine.

Because of early-morning fog and poor scouting, the Patriots did not detect Howe's flanking attack until it was too late. Howe and his chief general, Charles Cornwallis, led the Redcoats in an attack of the right rear of the American lines.

At first, there was much confusion. But then, after adjusting their lines of combat, the Patriots fought back furiously. Their artillery fire was especially effective. However, outmaneuvered and outgunned by the British, Washington's forces finally fell back. At several points it appeared that the Continental Army would be completely encircled and destroyed, but American General Nathanael Greene held off the British while Washington's forces staged an orderly, fighting retreat.

As the Americans fled the field of battle, they were pursued by the British until nightfall, when the fighting finally stopped. The day had been a disaster for the Patriots, who lost about 200 men killed, 500 wounded, and 400 captured. They also lost 11 cannons. The British suffered 89 killed and 488 wounded.

Washington's army was soundly beaten at Brandywine, but it remained intact. His men had shown tremendous fighting spirit, and morale remained high. In a report to the Continental Congress after the battle, Washington wrote, "Notwithstanding the misfortune of the day, I am happy to find the troops in good spirits; and I hope another time we shall compensate for the losses now sustained."

British General Howe had not expected such bitter resistance from the Patriots, and lost his chance to crush the enemy. For now, he would move his army closer to the main prize of the British assault: Philadelphia.

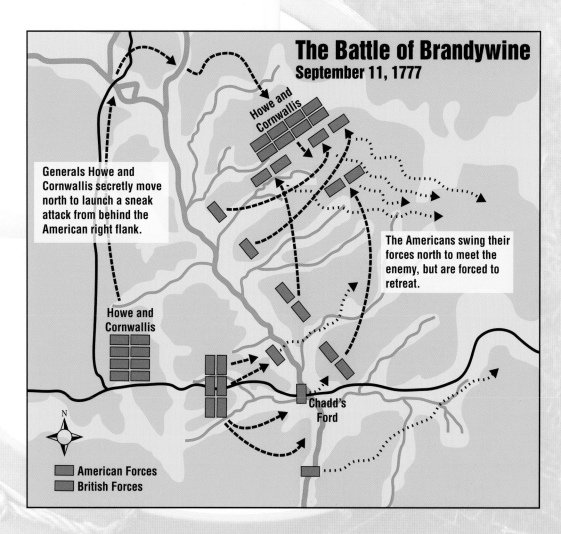

The Battle of Brandywine
September 11, 1777

Howe and Cornwallis

Generals Howe and Cornwallis secretly move north to launch a sneak attack from behind the American right flank.

The Americans swing their forces north to meet the enemy, but are forced to retreat.

Howe and Cornwallis

Chadd's Ford

N

American Forces
British Forces

October 4, 1777

THE BATTLE OF GERMANTOWN

For several days after the Battle of Brandywine, both the British and Continental Armies maneuvered and skirmished around each other in the Pennsylvania countryside. On the night of September 20, several thousand British troops attacked General Anthony Wayne's sleeping forces near Paoli, using bayonets and swords. The "Paoli Massacre" resulted in 53 Americans killed, 100 wounded, and 71 captured.

The Paoli Massacre

As British forces drew ever closer to Philadelphia, Pennsylvania, the Continental Congress finally abandoned the city, fleeing west to Lancaster, and then later to York, Pennsylvania.

On September 23, 1777, General Charles Cornwallis marched several British units into Philadelphia unopposed. Commander-in-Chief General William Howe had achieved his goal of capturing the rebel capital. Normally, such an event would have ended the war. But the Patriots had simply moved their government elsewhere, and George Washington's army was still intact and fighting. General Cornwallis moved the bulk of his forces, about 10,000 Redcoats, to the small village of Germantown, just five miles (8 km) north of colonial Philadelphia.

Stinging from the defeats at Brandywine and Paoli, George Washington boldly decided to turn the tables on Cornwallis. On October 4, he hurled 11,000 Patriots against the British defenders. The first assault drove the Redcoats back. But a thick morning fog and poor planning confused the attacking Americans. Their assault stalled when they failed to dislodge British soldiers from the Chew house, a stone structure from which the Redcoats could shoot at the Americans. Then, to make matters worse, Patriot units began accidentally firing on each other in the fog and musket smoke. The men panicked, and Washington was forced to call off the attack.

The Battle of Germantown was another American disaster. The Patriots lost 152 men killed, 521 wounded, and 400 captured. The British lost 71 killed, 450 wounded, and 14 captured. The British held their grip on Philadelphia. But once again, the American army left the field of battle intact, ready to fight another day. And far to the north, in New York state, events were unfolding that would have far-reaching consequences as a turning point in the American Revolution.

Americans attack the Chew house, a British stronghold during the Battle of Germantown, October 4, 1777.

September 19 and October 7, 1777

THE BATTLES OF SARATOGA

To regain control of the rebellious North American colonies, British General John Burgoyne devised a plan to isolate New England. The northern colonies were seen as the center of the American Revolution. Burgoyne and other British officials believed that if the "troublemakers" in New England were cut off, then the rest of the rebellion could be dealt with more easily.

New York's Lake Champlain and Hudson River were important water "highways" through the region. Trade goods and military supplies could easily be transported from Canada all the way to New York City, both of which were under British control in 1777.

Burgoyne's plan involved three parts. First, the general would personally command a huge invasion force traveling south from Canada into New York state. They would move first by boat over Lake Champlain, and then overland. After reaching the Hudson River, the army would continue south to Albany, New York.

A smaller expedition, commanded by Colonel Barry St. Leger, would depart from Lake Ontario and then push east along

CANADA

Lake Champlain

The 1777 British plan to invade New York.

Lake Ontario

Saratoga

NH

Mohawk River

Albany

NEW YORK

Hudson River

MASS.

PENNSYLVANIA

CONN.

NEW JERSEY

New York City

Atlantic Ocean

* Borders are present day

A cannon is perched on a hill at Saratoga Battlefield, New York.

the Mohawk River, linking up with Burgoyne's forces in Albany. Finally, a large part of General William Howe's army would move north from New York City. Burgoyne hoped that this three-pronged attack, called the "Northern Campaign," would split the colonies and make the rebels easier to defeat.

Burgoyne's plan was doomed to failure. General Howe, the commander in chief of British forces in North America, did not want to move the bulk of his forces north to help Burgoyne. He was busy capturing the rebel capital of Philadelphia, Pennsylvania. Howe left a small force in New York City under the command of General Henry Clinton. Clinton would try to help Burgoyne, but it would not amount to much.

On June 17, 1777, Burgoyne left Canada with a 9,000-man army and headed south. At first, the invasion went well. On July 6, the British recaptured the stronghold of Fort Ticonderoga on Lake Champlain. But rough terrain and limited supplies began to take their toll. Colonel St. Leger halted his push down the Mohawk River and retreated back to Canada. Burgoyne suffered a terrible loss in August at the Battle of Bennington, near the Vermont-New York border.

By September, the expedition was reduced to about 6,000 Redcoats still capable of fighting. Burgoyne pressed on, following the west bank of the Hudson River to a point just south of the town of Saratoga, New York. Here, he encountered a blocking force of about 7,000 Patriot soldiers. The Patriots were under the command of General Horatio Gates, who set up defensive positions, including artillery, on a piece of high ground called Bemis Heights.

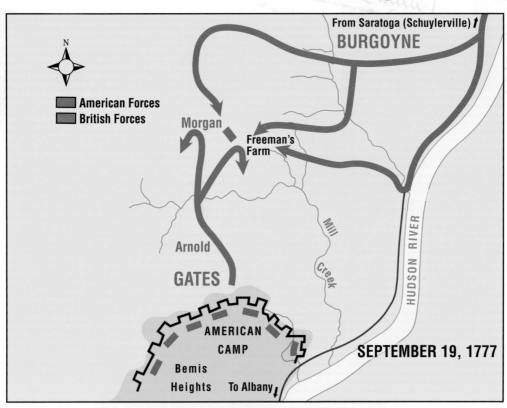

Colonel Daniel Morgan's riflemen, well adapted to the wooded terrain, took a fearful toll of British lives with their Kentucky rifles at the Battles of Saratoga.

On September 19, Burgoyne's army tried to go around the Americans. The British were met by stiff resistance by units led by Patriot commanders Daniel Morgan and Benedict Arnold. Much of the fighting took place in a clearing called Freeman's Farm. Cannons blazed, and furious British bayonet charges were thrown back by the Patriots. By the end of the day, the Americans retreated to their defensive positions on Bemis Heights. There, they waited for the British to make their next move.

Burgoyne's "victory" had come at a terrible price: more than 600 Redcoats killed, wounded, and captured. With their forces depleted and supplies running out, the British dug in. They waited for several weeks for reinforcements from New York City, but help never arrived.

General Burgoyne could have retreated back to Canada, but he decided instead to go on the attack again on October 7. The well-prepared American soldiers beat back the British. On the final assault before nightfall, Benedict Arnold rode into battle on horseback, leading his men to capture a British stronghold. He suffered a severe leg wound. If he had died that day, he would have become a hero for all time, one of the best leaders of the American army. Instead, the traitor Arnold later betrayed his country by joining the British.

The battle had resulted in another 600 British killed, wounded, and captured. The Patriots lost 150 killed or wounded. Under cover of night, Burgoyne led his battered army north, away from the Americans.

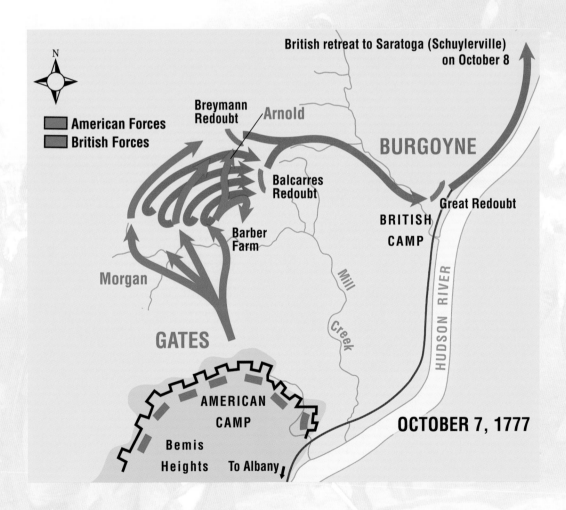

British General Burgoyne surrenders to General Washington on October 17, 1777, at Saratoga, New York.

But Patriot reinforcements came pouring in. By the time the exhausted British army limped to the outskirts of the town of Saratoga, they found themselves surrounded by more than 20,000 Patriots. On October 17, Burgoyne had no choice but to surrender his entire army to General Gates and the Americans.

News of the British surrender at Saratoga greatly helped the American cause. France, Great Britain's longtime enemy, threw its support behind the United States, officially recognizing the young country's independence. Within months, French troops, weapons, and ships would be arriving. Spain and the Netherlands would also soon join the Americans. But the war was far from over. In the south, George Washington and his Continental Army would first have to endure a terrible winter camp at Valley Forge, Pennsylvania.

VALLEY FORGE

After the British capture of Philadelphia, Pennsylvania, and the Patriot defeat at the Battle of Germantown in the autumn of 1777, General George Washington moved the Continental Army to winter quarters at Valley Forge, Pennsylvania. Named for a nearby iron forge, Valley Forge was just 18 miles (29 km) northwest of Philadelphia, and easily defendable.

The winter of 1777-1778 was bitterly cold and miserable. Washington's exhausted, hungry troops were poorly clothed and exposed to the elements. They chopped down trees to build hundreds of crude wooden huts. Unfortunately, the close quarters bred disease. During that cruel winter, more than 2,000 soldiers died of typhoid, dysentery, and pneumonia.

George Washington and the Continental Army faced severe conditions during the winter of 1777-1778.

Friedrich von Steuben trains Patriot troops during the winter of 1777-1778.

General Nathanael Greene, a former iron forge owner, created a new supply system for the Continental Army. He arranged for payments to outside businesses so that the troops were provided with sufficient food, ammunition, clothing, and animals.

In February 1778, Baron Friedrich von Steuben arrived at Valley Forge. The former Prussian officer had much experience in warfare. He tirelessly taught the troops proper drilling techniques.

He made them practice so much that soon the Patriots could follow orders like clockwork, and load and fire their muskets without thinking. Under Washington and von Steuben's guidance, the troops at Valley Forge were transformed into a formidable fighting force.

By spring, the French alliance with America became official. There was much rejoicing. With spirits soaring, Washington led his troops out of Valley Forge on June 19, 1778, ready to do battle once again with the British.

June 28, 1778
THE BATTLE OF MONMOUTH

On May 8, 1778, General William Howe was replaced by General Henry Clinton as commander in chief of British forces in North America. Fearing a French attack, General Clinton decided to pull all 10,000 of his troops from Philadelphia, Pennsylvania, and move them to defend New York City.

On June 28, on their way across the plains of central New Jersey, the Redcoats were attacked at Monmouth by George Washington and 12,000 troops of the Continental Army. In the blistering summer heat, both sides fought fiercely. George Washington personally led several attacks. At the end of the day, each side lost almost 400 men.

After nightfall, the British withdrew and sped to New York City. Monmouth was the last major battle fought in the north. It proved the fighting capability of the newly restored American army. Momentum was finally on the Patriots's side. Could they take advantage of their good fortune and win the war?

TIMELINE

DECEMBER 26, 1776
The Battle of Trenton is fought in New Jersey. The surprise attack led by George Washington marks a needed victory for the Patriots in the American Revolution.

JANUARY 3, 1777
The Battle of Princeton is fought in Princeton, New Jersey. Once again, Washington's troops defeat the Redcoats.

JANUARY 6, 1777
After two major victories, Washington and his troops set up winter quarters in Morristown, New Jersey.

SEPTEMBER 11, 1777
British Generals Howe and Cornwallis outmaneuver Washington's Continental Army, inflicting serious damage on the Patriots during the Battle of Brandywine.

SEPTEMBER 19, 1777
The first Battle of Saratoga, New York, is fought between British General Burgoyne's Redcoats and the Patriots, led by Daniel Morgan and Benedict Arnold. Burgoyne's "victory" came at a terrible cost in British troop and supply losses.

SEPTEMBER 20-21, 1777
British troops attack sleeping Patriots, killing and wounding many American soldiers in Pennsylvania's Paoli Massacre.

OCTOBER 4, 1777
The Battle of Germantown is another American disaster. Washington retreats.

OCTOBER 7, 1777
General Burgoyne attacks again during the second Battle of Saratoga. Well-prepared American forces beat the British.

OCTOBER 17, 1777
General Burgoyne surrenders his exhausted British army to Patriot General Gates.

WINTER 1777-1778
General Washington and his Continental Army make winter camp in Valley Forge, Pennsylvania. Friedrich von Steuben spends the months training the soldiers, creating a formidable Patriot force.

JUNE 28, 1778
British forces on their way from Pennsylvania to New York City are attacked at Monmouth, New Jersey, by Washington and his trained Continental Army. The fierce Battle of Monmouth will prove the fighting spirit of Americans.

The Battle of Monmouth on June 28, 1778.

GLOSSARY

ARTILLERY
Large weapons of war, such as cannons, mortars, and howitzers, that are used by military forces on land and at sea.

CONTINENTAL CONGRESS
Lawmakers who governed the 13 Colonies after they declared their independence from Great Britain.

DURHAM BOATS
Large, wooden, flat-bottomed boats used to transport heavy loads, such as barrels of grain or iron ore. They are often measured 60 feet (18 m) in length, and could carry about 17 tons (15 metric tons) of cargo.

FLANKING MANEUVER
A military term that describes attacking one or both sides of an enemy force. A successful flanking maneuver partially surrounds the enemy and limits maneuverability. It is also a severe psychological shock to enemy forces to be flanked. Panic often results, causing the enemy to flee the battlefield.

HESSIANS
Troops from several regions of today's Germany were often paid mercenaries who fought for the British military. They came from places such as Bavaria, Brunswick, Anhalt, Hesse-Cassel, and Hesse-Hanau. The two Hesse realms provided the most troops, so Americans referred to any German soldier as a "Hessian." About 30,000 Hessians served in North America during the American Revolution. They had a reputation, even among the British,

as being skilled and ruthless in battle. Thousands of Hessians, however, deserted and fought for the Americans. There were also many Americans of German decent who fought in the war.

MERCENARIES

People who fight in a military action for money, not because they believe in supporting a country or for a just cause.

MUSKET

A single-shot weapon, fired from the shoulder, that resembles a modern rifle. Muskets have smooth bores (the inside of the barrel). Their accuracy and range were limited, but a volley of muskets from a large group of soldiers could be quite deadly.

PATRIOTS

Colonists who rebelled against Great Britain during the American Revolution.

REDCOATS

The name that was often given to British soldiers because part of their uniform included a bright red coat.

REDOUBT

A fort, or system of trenches and raised earthen berms. Redoubts are used to protect troops against frontal attacks. During the American Revolution they were temporary defensive structures often constructed of logs, piled dirt, or stones and bricks.

WINTER QUARTERS

A location where troops of soldiers live and train during cold winter months, when fighting is postponed.

INDEX